Under My Feet

Trap-Door Spiders

Patricia Whitehouse

Heinemann Library
Chicago, Illinois

Customer Service 888-454-2279
Visit our website at www.heinemannlibrary.com

Designed by Sue Emerson, Heinemann Library; Page layout by Que-Net Media™
Printed and bound in the United States by Lake Book Manufacturing, Inc.
Photo research by Bill Broyles

08 07 06 05 04
10 9 8 7 6 5 4 3 2 1

Library of Congress Cataloging-in-Publication Data
Whitehouse, Patricia, 1958-
  Trap-door spiders / Patricia Whitehouse.
      v. cm. – (Under my feet)
Contents: Do trap-door spiders live here? – What are trap-door spiders? – What do trap-door spiders look like? – Where do trap-door spiders live? – What do trap-door spider homes look like? – How do trap-door spiders make their homes? – What is special about trap-door spider homes? – How do trap-door spiders use their traps? – When do trap-door spiders come out from underground? – Trap-door spider home map.
  ISBN 1-4034-4318-1 (HC), 1-4034-4327-0 (Pbk.)
  1. Trap-door spiders–Juvenile literature. [1. Trap-door spiders. 2. Spiders.] I. Title.
  QL458.4.W477 2003
  595.4'4–dc21

2002156758

Acknowledgments
The author and publishers are grateful to the following for permission to reproduce copyright material:
p. 4 Jack Ballard/Visuals Unlimited; p. 5 Dr. Paul A. Zahl/Photo Researchers, Inc.; p. 6 Paul Freed/Animals Animals; p. 7 Bucky Reeves/Photo Researchers, Inc.; p. 8 David T. Roberts/Nature's Images, Inc./Photo Researchers, Inc.; p. 9 Pascal Goetgheluck/Ardea London Ltd.; pp. 10, 19 Oxford Scientific Film; p. 11L Corbis; p. 11R C. McIntyre/PhotoLink/Getty Images; pp. 12, 15, 16, 17B Fredrick Coyle; p. 13 Louis Quin/Photo Researchers, Inc.; p. 14 Michael Fogden/DRK Photo; p. 17T Lenny S. Vincent; p. 18 Gilbert Grant/Photo Researchers, Inc.; p. 20 Tony Mercieca/Photo Researchers, Inc.; p. 21 A. Cosmos Blank/Photo Researchers, Inc.; p. 23 (row 1, L-R) Paul Freed/Animals Animals, C. McIntyre/PhotoLink/Getty Images, Louis Quin/Photo Researchers, Inc.; (row 2, L-R) Fredrick Coyle, Paul Freed/Animals Animals, Fredrick Coyle; (row 3, L-R) Heinemann Library, Michael Fogden/DRK Photo; back cover (L-R) Fredrick Coyle, Michael Fogden/DRK Photo

Illustration on page 22 by Will Hobbs
Cover photograph by Oxford Scientific Films

Special thanks to our advisory panel for their help in the preparation of this book:

Alice Bethke, Library Consultant
Palo Alto, CA

Eileen Day, Preschool Teacher
Chicago, IL

Kathleen Gilbert,
Second Grade Teacher
Round Rock, TX

Sandra Gilbert,
Library Media Specialist
Fiest Elementary School
Houston, TX

Jan Gobeille,
Kindergarten Teacher
Garfield Elementary
Oakland, CA

Angela Leeper,
Educational Consultant
Wake Forest, NC

Special thanks to Dr. William Shear, Department of Biology, Hampden-Sydney College, for his review of this book.

Some words are shown in bold, **like this.**
You can find them in the picture glossary on page 23.

Contents

Do Trap-Door Spiders Live Here?

When you walk outside, you might not see a trap-door spider.

But you might be walking over one.

Trap-door spiders live under your feet.

Their homes are underground.

What Are Trap-Door Spiders?

exoskeleton

Trap-door spiders are **arachnids.**

Arachnids have a hard outside called an **exoskeleton.**

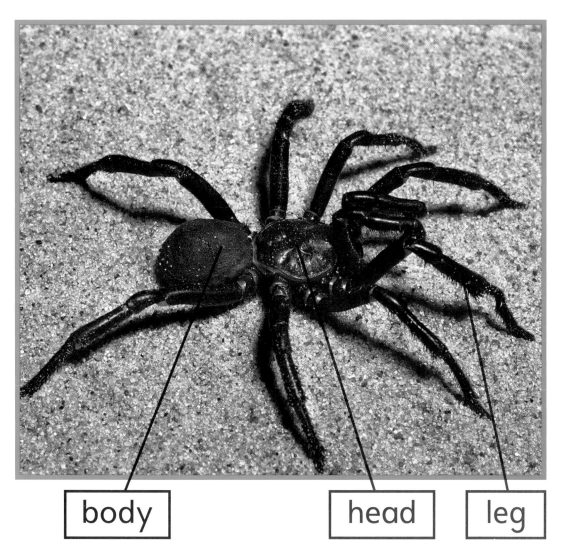

body   head   leg

Trap-door spiders have eight legs.

They have a head and a body.

What Do Trap-Door Spiders Look Like?

Most trap-door spiders are brown.

Trap-door spiders have hairs on their **exoskeleton**.

Trap-door spiders are about as long as a paper clip.

Where Do Trap-Door Spiders Live?

Most trap-door spiders live where it is warm all year.

Some trap-door spiders live where it is wet and rainy.

But most live in **deserts**.

What Do Trap-Door Spider Homes Look Like?

Trap-door spider **burrows** have long, thin **tunnels**.

The tunnels are about the size of a carrot.

door

The burrows are lined with spider **silk**.

A special door covers the burrow.

How Do Trap-Door Spiders Make Their Homes?

fang

Trap-door spiders use their **fangs** to dig their **burrows**.

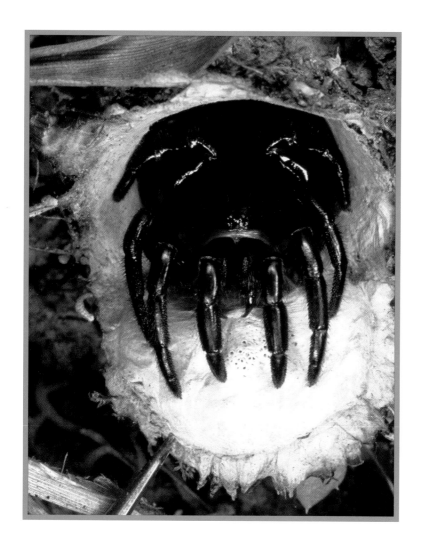

They make the doors with their **silk.**

Some trap-door spiders hide the door with leaves or dirt.

What Is Special About Their Homes?

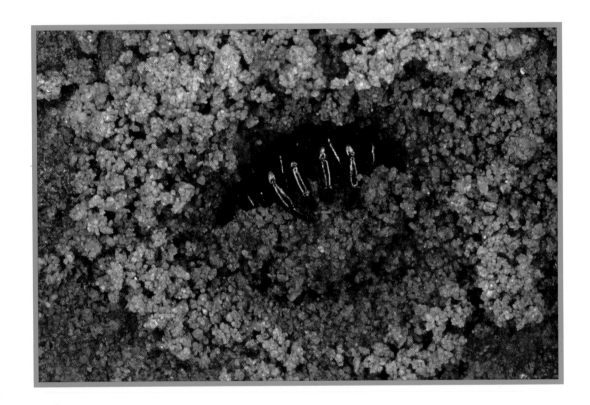

Trap-door spider homes can have different kinds of doors.

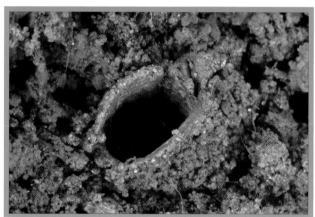

Some doors are thick, like a **cork**.

Some are thin, like paper.

How Do Trap-Door Spiders Use Their Traps?

Most trap-door spiders hold their doors shut with their **fangs.**

They feel if a bug is walking on their door.

Then, they open the door and grab the bug with their fangs.

When Do Trap-Door Spiders Come Out from Underground?

Sometimes trap-door spiders come out to catch bugs.

They may chase bugs that
run away.

But they do not go far from
their homes.

Trap-Door Spider Home Map

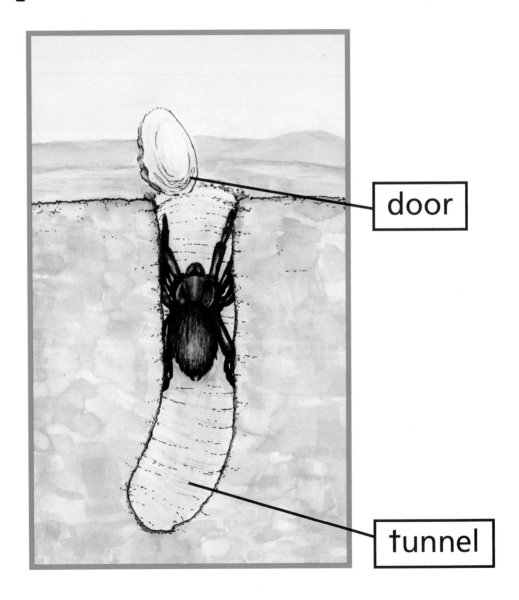

door

tunnel

Picture Glossary

arachnid
page 6

desert
page 11

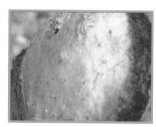

silk
pages 13, 15

burrow
pages 12, 13, 14

exoskeleton
pages 6, 8

tunnel
pages 12, 22

cork
page 17

fangs
pages 14, 18, 19

Note to Parents and Teachers

Reading for information is an important part of a child's literacy development. Learning begins with a question about something. Help children think of themselves as investigators and researchers by encouraging their questions about the world around them. Each chapter in this book begins with a question. Read the question together. Look at the pictures. Talk about what you think the answer might be. Then read the text to find out if your predictions were correct. Think of other questions you could ask about the topic, and discuss where you might find the answers. Assist children in using the picture glossary and the index to practice new vocabulary and research skills.

 CAUTION: Remind children that it is not a good idea to handle wild animals or insects. Children should wash their hands with soap and water after they touch any animal.

Index